MISSING LINK?

MISSING LINK?

Parent Discussions about Their Role in the Education of their Children

MATTIE LEE SOLOMON, PhD

iUniverse, Inc.
Bloomington

Missing Link?
Parent Discussions about Their Role in the Education of their Children

iUniverse books may be ordered through booksellers or by contacting:

iUniverse
1663 Liberty Drive
Bloomington, IN 47403
www.iuniverse.com
1-800-Authors (1-800-288-4677)

ISBN: 978-1-4620-5391-9 (sc)
ISBN: 978-1-4620-5392-6 (ebk)

Printed in the United States of America

iUniverse rev. date: 09/26/2011

To my daughter, Norma Deloris.
Watching you raise your daughter has been a pleasure.
I am proud of you.

Giving up on parents is giving up on an important link to the social and academic success of children.

Dr. M. L. Solomon

When you go through deep waters, I will be with you. When you go through rivers of difficulty, you will not drown. When you walk through the fire of oppression, you will not be burned up; the flames will not consume you.

Isaiah 43:2

TABLE OF CONTENTS

TABLE OF CONTENTS

ACKNOWLEDGMENT

With deepest gratitude, I want to thank the many parents across the state of Indiana who volunteered their time to have a conversation with me concerning how they felt about the way their children are being educated and their role in the process. I thank each of you for your honesty and for sharing the challenges you face.

I give a special thank-you to those who provided opportunities for me to meet with parents.

Most of all, I am grateful to the One through whom all things are possible.

INTRODUCTION

When I turned eighteen, I became the mother of a beautiful baby girl. I felt that I was prepared to be a mom because I knew how to change a baby's diaper and how to feed her. I was twenty-three when my daughter started kindergarten; I then realized that I did not know how to extend being a mom at home to being a parent who supported the educational process of my child at her school. I did know that I loved my daughter and wanted the best for her; however, I had not received any training or advice on how to become linked to this important part of her life. I now know that even though I did not know what to do, I was quietly being held accountable.

I came from generations of parents who kept everything to themselves, including how to support their child's education. This may have been because they could not pass on to us what had not been passed to them. When parents my age talked about their children, it was mostly about how to make them behave. The important thing for us was that our child did not embarrass us in public. My daughter is now grown with a child of her own, and we have many discussions about the challenges I faced as a parent during her educational process.

As a teacher and school administrator, I had many opportunities to have discussions with parents concerning their role in the education of their children. Although, I did not document those conversations, I knew how important they were. The discussions provided important insight into how their personal circumstances and challenges in life affected the link they had or did not have with the education of their children. After taking an early retirement from school administration, I wanted to continue to dialogue with parents. I feel that it is important for parents to have an avenue to discuss how they feel and to share their perspectives with other parents and educators. Writing *Missing Link?* provided this avenue.

The parents interviewed in *Missing Link?* are not parents I had contact with as a teacher or school administrator. They are parents who accepted an invitation to have a discussion about their perspectives of their children's education. I gained contact with these parents during various situations or from someone who had contact with parents via church or public service. One-on-one interviews and/or small group discussions were not set about methodically. My goal was to serve as an objective observer—not to advance an opinion but to collect feedback.

Parents interviewed were of all age groups and social and economic statuses. There were also many guardians who were in the role of parents of school-age children. Many relatives who have guardianship of children in school, such as grandparents, uncles, aunts, and siblings, have been thrust into the role of parents. In *Missing Link?*, all who have the responsibilities of raising school-age children will be called parents.

When it comes to the challenges parents face, I have found that parents explain their experiences the best. It is important that parents communicate with each other as well as those who are linked to their children's social and academic development. Raising children is a journey best not traveled alone. The mistakes can be costly and sometimes irreversible.

What happens in the home has a great deal to do with the way a child views the outside world and society. What happens in the home also has a direct effect on the way a child responds to his environment. It is for this reason that the viewpoint of the parent has to be taken seriously. The perspective of the parent is valuable when answering the question "What can educators do to improve student achievement?"

How parents feel about their children's education has to be known before we can take the necessary steps to involve them. The responsibility to develop children socially as well as academically cannot be one-sided, and passing the blame will not solve this dilemma. *Missing Link?* will provide insight from parents obtained during conversations and interviews about this dilemma and more.

Are parents the missing link to their children's social and academic progress? After conducting one-on-one interviews with parents and guardians, I found that parents had strong viewpoints, but some did not know how to articulate their feelings. This may have been because they had never been asked to have a conversation about their perspectives. For this reason, I used limited quotes in *Missing Link?*

Information concerning the perspectives of parents and what they value has to come from parents. There cannot be speculation about how parents feel because parents' views sometimes differ from those of the people educating their children. We have to meet them where they are in life.

As stated earlier, I decided to write *Missing Link?* as an avenue to more discussions with parents and to get a deeper understanding and insight about how they feel. This is not an attempt to answer questions for the reader; instead, it is an attempt to share parents' perspectives about how their children are being educated and their role in that process.

As a parent, when I was asked to complete a survey from my child's school, my responses to the survey questions were mostly influenced by what my daughter perceived as a good experience or a bad experience at school. All I had to go on were the stories that she would share with me about her day.

The many discussions with parents in *Missing Link?* are attempts to get parents to go beyond what they hear from their children. They are challenged to describe their feelings based on their personal experience and interactions with the school. As a school administrator, I was faced with the dilemma of how to get parents involved when, in fact, many parents may have felt that they *were* involved.

The following chapters are the result of discussions with parents on several topics concerning parents' link to their children's education. First we will discuss the parents' answer to the question "Do you feel that parents are missing in the educational process of their children?" Next we will reveal the following discussions concerning why schools have a hard time getting parents linked to their child's education. Discussions included topics such as empowering parents, who is responsible when a child fails in school, and what the responsibilities of parents are concerning the schooling of their children.

Missing Link? is the result of many conversations and one-on-one interviews with parents, with the goal of summarizing and sharing their perspectives of their children's education with you, the reader.

Missing Link? will provide a better understanding of how parents feel about the role they play as a link in the chain of their children's social and academic success.

The chain of social and academic success for children has many links: the parents, school, community, and church. All of the links have to be present and strong. If there is a weak or missing link, the child's chance for success is in jeopardy.

It has been said that parents are today's missing link. It is for this reason that a discussion with parents about their perspectives concerning their children's education and their role is so valuable and necessary. *Missing Link?* can be used as a conversational tool to stimulate discussions for parents and educators.

CHAPTER ONE

THE MISSING LINK

Do parents view their involvement in the educational process of their children the same way educators do? If not, does this difference in viewpoint cause parents to be perceived as missing in the educational process by educators? Parents discussed these observations and many other matters related to the factors that affect how parents view the educational process of their children and how their view of these issues affects their children's views. How parents think and feel about education has an effect on how their children think and feel about education as well.

Other issues found to disconnect or link parents to their children's education are income status, educational level, and generational issues in families.

Parents openly discussed with me some of the reasons that they feel parents are missing in their children's education. One major reason given was that parents may not know what to do or how to help.

A parent of two children in elementary school stated: "Yes, parents are missing; if they don't have an education and the benefits that come with being educated, how can they encourage their children?"

Other than showing up for the Parent-Teacher Organization meetings, some parents do not know the next step. Parents felt that it's hard to be a part of their children's educational process if they don't know anything about it.

They also felt that parents have not been taught how to support their children's education and have no idea what their role should be at school.

Most moms and dads will make an effort to show up at ball games and even to see their child perform in a play or sing in the school choir. Parents perceived that parents were missing except for these types of activities. They felt that the schools should add parent training programs to the agenda during these events.

Are children who have both the mother and father present in the home at an advantage because the parents can support each other? When asked this question, parents said that this is not always true.

A mother of four said that when it comes to their children's education, her husband is missing. "Because his mother was a single mom, he watched her do everything concerning her kids, and he feels that I should as well. So I have to take up the responsibility of making sure one of us stays connected to what is going on with our children's education."

Another parent stated that his mother valued education but his father did not; he believed in hard work and was street-smart. "He was not educated but told us that we had to finish high school, and we were afraid not to finish high school." But when he did finish, his father was not at his graduation. This experience left him with a mixed message from his parents. He feels that parents have to be the ones to push the child. He also shared that one of his children has a learning challenge and so he is more lax with him concerning his school assignments than he is with his daughter, and his daughter became angry with him because he pushed her and not her brother. He said that maybe he needs to take another look at how he is handling this situation because, "I don't want to send mixed messages about the importance of education to my children the way my parents did to my sisters, brothers, and I."

Knowing what is going on in the educational system is a challenge for some parents. As one parent said, "Education is always changing, upgrading or evolving. Keeping up with the educational system seems to be a problem for many parents. They feel intimidated and do not always discuss this issue with the school."

One area in which they feel school districts have upgraded or evolved is the way they communicate with parents. Parents are contacted by an automated telephone system. A recorded message is sent out by the school to give information about events and school closings. Although the parents said that they do not have a problem with this method of communication, they feel that it has taken away from the need to have a personal relationship with the school.

A teacher said that she felt her students' parents were linked with the school because they communicated with her on daily basis by e-mail, the school's website, in the car when they picked up the students, and when they signed off on journals sent home by the students. Her school provided laptop computers for parents to use, and the principal did home visits to help the parents set up the computers. She stated that, as a parent, she felt that communication was the key and that using technology to communicate was one way to do it, and she was okay with it.

An elementary education school worker and parent shared that she found that parents were uninvolved or missing in their children's education. "There is a vicious cycle of parents who are uneducated, and education is not important in the family."

Is it true that low-income parents do not have high expectations for their children education? One parent explained how she felt by sharing the following remarks: "I don't believe that income is the determining factor in how parents view their children's education. To generally say that low-income parents don't hold high expectations is untrue. I myself was raised by a single parent who, at a particular time, was on welfare. Education was a high priority for our family. All of us (my two siblings and I) have college degrees. Two of us have graduate degrees. Low income/poverty does not equal failure. High expectations lead to higher achievement."

A parent who has a nine-year-old son in elementary school felt that there was a difference in how low-income parents versus high-income parents viewed their children's education. In the words of this parent: "Parents who have a high income usually are educated or have worked really hard to get where they are. Therefore, they pass on to their children the knowledge and experience it takes to be successful. Those parents understand the value of education and that education is an investment. They also position their children to receive the knowledge and experience that it will take to be successful. For example, they put their children in good schools, in great programs and activities. In contrast, parents who have low incomes most often depend on federal assistance or work in low paying jobs. They may not have experienced enough success in their own education or the work place to pass on these skills/values to their children. Therefore, they value money more than education because money is tangible and is felt when it's scarce."

The perception of a parent who has a child in high school is that parents need to invest in their children's education. This parent said, "You would think low-income parents would care more so that their children would make a better life for themselves and end the generational poverty. However, they don't care as much because they are living in survival mode. They are just trying to get their basic needs met. High-income parents know that it is possible to attain goals, and hold their children to a higher standard. Higher-income parents send their kids to private schools. They are more financially invested in their children's future."

No matter what the circumstances are for the families, parents perceive that it is about holding someone accountable. Parents also shared that in certain aspects the parents are missing. Most all of the parents I spoke with felt that parents with low incomes don't understand the power of influence they have on their children and on the educational system.

One teacher and parent of a child in middle school felt that parents should speak up. "They are often too quiet on important educational issues involving their children. They may relate their income to the value of their vote. They also are not visible in our schools."

Parents felt that, like low-income parents, parents with high incomes are not very visible because they have time-consuming jobs; however, they are not quiet on educational issues and speak out loudly. They want the best for their children because they feel they make a big contribution through their taxes.

A parent who shared that she and her husband earned what can be considered a high income had the following perspective: "I think that all family situations are different. There are parents of low and high income levels who are not linked to the educational process of their children, and the same can be said for those who are linked. It depends on whether or not they value education."

Does the parent's need to be linked with his or her child's school lessen after elementary school? Parents said that their child's elementary school years were more crucial, but once the child is in middle school, there is more concern about his behavior because he is going through some serious hormonal changes and most children do not have control over their emotions.

One parent said, "I don't know if it is less. I think that it depends on how much the child is interested in school and whether or not the child has behavior issues. I have three boys, and they are good kids. I don't have to check on them as much as when they were in elementary school. One of my sons, who is in the tenth grade, has English and reading problems, so I do check with his teachers concerning his progress. I also do my part at home with him by having him read and write about what he read, and I check it and make the reading assignment a part of his allowance."

It is important to wean children slowly, parents felt, because once they leave the elementary level, cutting children off too quickly would affect them in a negative way and they may interpret this to mean that the parents no longer care. Parents are not missing after elementary school; they feel that they do not need to be there in the same way. However, some parents felt that this was a mistake because even when children are older, they need just as much attention to stay on track—sometimes more. Parent-teacher communication is even more important because the parent and teacher should work together to solve any issues that are keeping the child from being successful in school, including correcting the child's behavior.

One mother gave the following input: "As children grow up, we parents teach them to be more independent and to start taking more responsibility for their schoolwork. My son works hard and tries to stay out of trouble because he knows that if he doesn't, I will be at the school. To boys it's as un-cool to have Mom show up at school when you are thirteen as it is when you are five or six."

Another parent felt that as the child gets older, there are less learning activities that require parents to be engaged at home. She said, "In elementary school, the child needs or requires more help with homework, projects, and other learning activities. As the child gets older, parents perceive less time is needed in this manner. As a parent, it seems to me that communication from the teacher to the parent declines as well. My daughter is in the tenth grade. Out of all of her teachers, I only receive communication regarding her progress from two. Even these are not very regular. When I attended the parent/teacher conference, only one teacher, the dance instructor, gave me very tangible ways to help my daughter at home."

A parent of a seventeen-year-old daughter felt that parents are linked to children's educational process in elementary school more because they feel their children are still dependent on them for security. "In elementary, they are doing a lot of milestone things, such as their first play and first musical. As children get older, parents tend to loosen the grip more and give them more independence. Their education is just as important, but we feel that we have established them with the school routine and instilled some of the basic values so we don't have to be at the school once a week anymore."

One educator and parent described how she is on both sides of the fence by saying, "Often I see myself in the parents' shoes. I feel parents work so hard to provide their children with the necessities that they rely heavily on the teacher for feedback. Since my job required so much of my time, it was hard to find time to visit or check up on my son. As an educator, I always encourage parents to visit my class so they can see what goes on and how their children respond to my teaching. Then, I recognized I had to start eating my own words. My argument was that my son is a good student;

however, I realized that he valued positive feedback from me, his parent, way more than his teacher. I began to see him responding better to me visiting his class, just to hang out, than coming to talk to his teacher just when he was in trouble or for parent/teacher conferences. My presence in his classroom has made a big difference. My son is not a bad student, but he loves to see me in the class."

In the next chapter, parents share their perspectives concerning getting linked to their children's educational process. They discuss things that they feel do and do not link them effectively, and why.

CHAPTER TWO

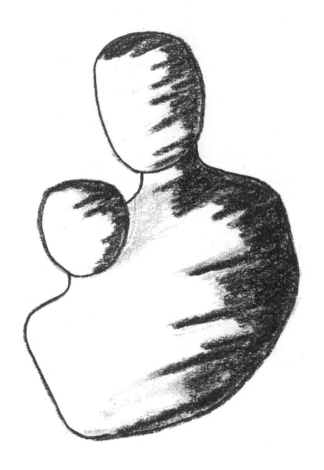

GETTING PARENTS LINKED

Some parents feel that they are so caught up with everyday life that they don't find they have time to engage in their children's education. Low-income parents are concerned with providing the basic needs of their children. One parent stated that just making sure basic needs are met for her children can be overwhelming. However, being preoccupied with life situations and circumstances is not only an issue with low-income parents. As alluded to in the previous chapter, many parents I spoke with felt caught up or preoccupied with some aspect of life, such as paying bills, job pressures, and health issues. Parents also felt that being busy with other children and time restraints kept some of them from being linked to what is going on with their children's education. There are other parents who said that no matter what, parents should make time to be involved in every aspect of their children's life, and they shared why they feel this is important.

A police officer and parent of a fourteen-and seventeen-year-old stated that he and his wife have always been involved through all grade levels of their children's education. An example he gave of their teamwork: when his daughter was accepted into the college of her choice, he and his wife went to every meeting and college event with her. He also said, "We work as a team. My wife and I saw kids being dropped off by their parents and noticed that some parents chose to let them do things on their own. I feel that it is important for the school and the staff to know that the parents are involved, and the parents should have high expectations for not only the child but for the school."

During our one-on-one discussion, a father of four children shared that he felt that I needed to know a little about his background to fully understand his present perspectives on his children's education and his role in it. He said that his feelings were tied to how his parents felt about education and that the link was broken when he and his nine siblings were in school. He has tried to repair the damage with his children.

This parent shared that his family was poor, mother had a sixth-grade education and his father had none. His mother taught his father how to write his name. He could do math in his head, and because he had a photographic memory, people thought that he could read. When he was little, his mother would help him read. She would also help him with words he could not pronounce, but he said that as he got older and she had more kids (nine), she did not have the time to spend with him.

Despite the fact that he made straight A's in school, his teachers thought that he was having academic problems. He felt that they did not recognize his academic success because they were focused on the poverty condition that his family was in. His family did not have anything. The school fed them with leftover food from the cafeteria. He and his sibling had bad teeth and no clothes, and because of this, the school staff thought he was an academic special needs student. "They thought that I could not learn because my family was poor."

He said that the teachers in the school he attended were mostly young white teachers who did not know anything about his culture and that although they tried to help feed his family they had not been taught how to link his parents to his education.

Parents were not sure what type of training, if any, the schools provide for teachers concerning parents, but felt that the parents should be included in the training. They shared that they are mostly contacted by the school when children misbehave or get hurt and that during teacher meetings, the teachers take the lead in the conversation and the parents are not asked what type of support they need.

As one parent said, "During parent/teacher conferences, they tell us why they feel the child is passing or failing. In most cases, the child is either completing his class work and homework or he is not."

Several parents said that they feel frustrated because sometimes they cannot help with homework because they do not understand it themselves. They are embarrassed to tell the teacher that they do not have the knowledge needed to help with school assignments.

Does how parents feel about education affect how their children view education? A Father of a high school student replied: "That is huge! Parents have to show that they value education by talking to their child about the importance of good grades and going to college. My wife and I always talk to our children about college. We let them know that there are no ifs, ands, or buts. They are going to college. We set the bar by being linked to their educational process. We also reward them when they do well with grades and citizenship."

Another parent said, "If parents feel education is important, they will instill those values in their children. Also, they will be more involved in assisting their child with homework and making sure that he attends school regularly. I think it is imperative that parents are active in their child's education and lead by example."

A fifty-seven-year-old mother of three grown children who is currently in school trying to complete her high school education stated that she promised her grandchildren that she would get her diploma. She shared the following about her life: "My parents were uneducated, and of my three children, only one completed high school. I feel that I was affected by my parents not finishing school, and my not finishing was passed on to my children. I am hoping that my going to back school now will make a difference to my grandchildren."

She also shared that in the past she could always get a job. She said that some years ago, she worked in a factory for ten years and made what she felt was good money, but now she can't get a job. She felt that this was not because of her age but because she does not have a high school diploma.

Parents shared that some parents just don't realize how important parent involvement is. They are consumed with their lives and problems, and they overlook the children's education. Parents also felt that there was a lack of resources for the parents.

Is it beginning to sound like parents have many explanations for why they are not linked with their children's education? When asked if there are any good excuses or reasons not to know what is going on with your children, all stated "no." They realized that they have to find a way to balance things out. Parents admit that they need help. It would help if the schools could offer classes, such as budgeting finances and time management for parents. They stated that some parents need to learn parenting skills, and that parenting skills consist of more than learning about academics and how to read test scores.

One parent said that she was frustrated because, "When the state test ISTEP is given to my child's school, they schedule a time to discuss the results with parents. I understand the importance of ISTEP but feel that I cannot do anything to help after the fact."

As stated earlier, the parents' frame of mind and focus is reflected onto their children. The children bring what their parents are going through at home to school with them each day.

A state police officer and parent of two school age children stated that: "Parents who set higher educational standards for their children usually have high-achieving students who have education as a top priority. Parent satisfaction with the school also affects the child and how they feel about education. If a parent is highly satisfied, it will manifest itself in the child's performance and behavior in a positive way."

In order to create an effective parent and school connection one parents felt that there is a need to feel welcomed when they visit the school. "The schools should make the parents feel that they care about them and what they go through, and give them the support they need."

They perceived that being made to feel welcomed in the school would replace the occasional feelings that they are being blamed and not understood. One parent stated that when she spoke to the school about her child's failing grades, she felt that they couldn't care less about her and so she began to shut down and feel helpless and overpowered in the situation. Another parent who felt very welcome at her children's school stated that: "The principal and teachers are good at keeping me informed. They return my phone calls, and when I visit the school, they call me by name and they know my child's name."

Being linked with their children's education was also important to parents because they felt that this meant knowing their child's teacher, school policies and politics, and volunteering when they could so that they could meet other parents.

According to a parent of a college student, parents should make themselves known in their child's school. "You know you are linked when important people in the school (i.e., principal, teachers, and counselors) can put your face with your name. This happens when you participate in activities, such as visiting the classroom, helping with homework, and going to parent and teacher conferences."

Other activities parents mentioned were reading to their children's class and being a member of parent groups. Parents also believe that being linked means knowing who your children are and what they are involved in. This means taking the time to listen and learn their interest. Sometimes it's pushing the issue until communication happens. Parents said that they should be helping the children be successful in getting an education and that when they are involved their children realize that they care about them. Most important, it lets children know that they support their education, sport events, or whatever they are doing. One parent said, "If we as parents don't care, our children will be affected by our attitude and will develop a negative attitude toward school and sometimes even life. It is up to the home to keep children motivated. In the school setting, parent involvement should be that of the observer. The school system should be set up to thoroughly educate the child, and reinforcement should happen at home."

It is crucial for parents to realize that the link with their children's education also has an effect on their emotional and physical well-being. Parents felt that this is important because it is directly related to how successful children are in all areas of their life.

They also feel that for some parents, education, for varied reasons, is not a priority. Therefore, their participation in their children's education is lacking. For single parents, this may be because they work and are unable to make parent-teacher meetings or other activities that are usually set during the school day or right when they are still trying to get off work. As stated earlier, some parents, single or otherwise, just are not aware of how to best be involved and support education at home.

One single dad who I spoke with shared that when his two-year-old daughter attends school, he will be her first teacher. He feels that he set the example of how and what she can expect out of life. "I am her protector and I will be involved from the beginning with her education. She will be aware of my presence even when I am not there because she will know that I may come to the school at any time. Some students are not focused, so they are lost. It is the parents' responsibility to help their children stay focused."

Another single parent who shared that he is preparing his son for preschool felt that parents need to monitor what their children are being taught. "Ever since he was six months old, I have said his A, B, and Cs with him every day. I know there are toys that will do this but I feel that it is important for me to do it. My parents read to us, and Mom did not allow anyone to use baby talk when they were talking to her children. I feel that parents need to make the time needed to monitor what their children are being taught and spend productive time with them."

Being linked to children's education through knowledge and communication is powerful. The discussions in the following chapter will attest to what parents feel will empower them and why they need to be empowered concerning their children's education.

CHAPTER THREE

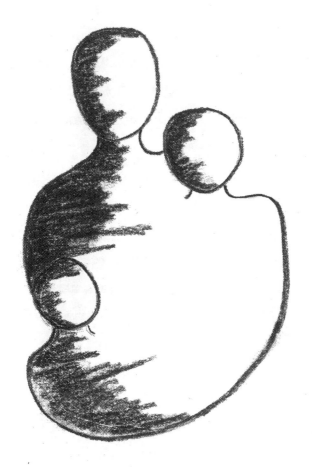

EMPOWERING PARENTS

Research has been done for decades by educators across America and the world to answer the question "How can we improve parental involvement?" The answer to this question has been linked to student academic success, discipline, and attendance issues. I asked parents what they can do to empower themselves to be a positive link in the educational process of their children. Many parents felt that a question parents should ask themselves is "If we do not get involved with our children, why should we expect the schools to take up our issues?"

I began our discussion by explaining what I felt being *empowered* means. It means more than just being involved with school programs, such as athletics. Being empowered means that they know how to effect the necessary changes and demands that will influence the educational process of their children and ensure that effective academic and social developmental strategies are being implemented in the school.

One of the things parents felt was necessary was that there should be more conversations by schools with parents about how parents feel about their children's education, and that schools should empower parents to educate and evaluate their children. Steps should be taken to bridge the gap of communication by meeting parents where they are and not assuming that because a parent does not come or call frequently, they don't care.

Communication was one way many of the parents I spoke with felt they could be empowered. They stated that all forms of communication, such as calls, letters, e-mails, and internet, would be helpful. Effective, consistent, and informative communication is the key. A parent who felt that parents should not be surprised when a child bring home a bad report card also stated that: "There should be communication with the parent at the first sign of failure so that the problem can be identified and corrected, whether it is a home or school issue."

Another parent shared that communication is powerful. "I think the schools just need to stay in constant communication with the parents. I like the web grades where you can check your child's progress at any moment. I like the automated calls I receive when my child misses class. I also think that in high school, the school counselor should meet with the parents and a student to discuss the student's educational progress; this type of communication is powerful."

The perspective of parents is that they should also be educated on the positive results of their involvement. Parents have different means, abilities, and needs; the school can create classes for the parent based on this information. The school should also have strict rules for students and parents.

Parents agree that there should be consequences not only for students who break the rules but for parents as well.

To become better informed to the educational process, parents felt that they needed to be asked what their needs are and have help given to them that would train them to be more connected to their kid's education. They felt that some parents may have to break the generational curse of their parents and grandparents, who were not involved in their children's education, and that maybe the church could also be the link for spiritual guidance for them in this area.

One grandmother who is the guardian of her daughter's school age children said, "If there are no past role models for parents in their family, they do not know what it is to be empowered to support their children's education. They have not had an example of how to communicate effectively with the school, and this can be intimidating and cause the link to be broken or never happen."

I invited a twenty-year-old guardian to have a discussion with me concerning her perspectives as a guardian. This young adult has taken over guardianship of her sister's teenage daughter. She now has the legal responsibility of a parent for her niece's health, security, and education. During our discussion concerning empowering parents, she shared that the school her niece attends does not take her wanting to be involved in her educational process seriously. She said that her relationship with the school started out with a lack of communication from the teachers, but it soon got better when she started showing up at the school regularly she also shared that: "When you are having a grown-up life while people see others your age partying, it is hard for them to take your role as a concerned parent to a teenager seriously. I know I am a parent and I need to have the same power that other parents have, because I influence my niece's dreams and visions the same way they do for their children. I have high expectations for my niece."

This guardian continued by sharing that there was a problem when she discovered that her expectations concerning educational issues were different from her niece's biological mother and her family. She felt that when you get a child who has some years and you do not know the history of the child, this can cause you to be unprepared to make the necessary decisions concerning her education and other issues.

She added that: "My niece had been told that she was doing well in school. I found that doing well to her mother and other members of my family was a 2.0 GPA and issues with fighting the other students when things did not go her way. I not only need to be empowered by the school but also by my family if I am going to turn this young lady around. No one has truly sat down with me and wanted to know what I am going through. No one knows the sacrifice you make with a child; they only see the product."

As one parent compared parents of the fifties, sixties, and seventies to modern parents, he felt that today's parents are disconnected. He also felt that the disconnection may have happened because "the neighborhoods have changed" and the black family he knew has changed. He said, "We have turned away from being a spiritual group of people and have allowed the media to dictate how we bring up our children. My parents are in their late fifties, and during their day, there were partnerships with families and schools. The school knew the family would discipline and do their part, but today's modern day parents expect the school to be both parent and instructor, and they do not see anything wrong with it. Black educated people moving out of their neighborhoods could also be a cause, because the children do not see examples of all the different professions that people who look like them and come from the same place are involved in."

A parent who has three children in school, one at each grade level—elementary, middle school, and high school—felt that parents are empowered by getting to know their children's teachers, counselors, and coaches. They should read the information the school sends home, and ask questions of the school and their children. She also shared that parents cannot be lazy when it comes to the hard work it takes making sure their children are getting the proper education she concluded that: "If parents teach their children to respect authority, work hard, and value education, the children will model that. If a parent is lazy and apathetic, children will model that as well."

When asked about how they as parents could be empowered, two parents perspectives were as follows: "The more I know about my son's teachers and how they operate their classrooms, the more I am empowered. I like to know his/her teaching methods, his/her expectations for my child, and how my son responds to him/her. I learn these things by visiting the classroom, communicating often with his teachers, and communicating with my son. I also like to know about the school's performance as a whole, what programs they offer, and the type of diversity of the staff. Knowledge is power; so, the more I know about the teacher, the school, and the school district, the more it empowers me to be involved in my son's education. Parents have more power of influence then they know".

The other parent felt that whether they value education or not, the lack of involvement will have a negative effect on their children, but when they are involved they have a positive effect she shared that they teach their children principles, such as diligence, good work ethics, effort, consistency, and that education is an investment worth more than fast cash. They do this by making sure their children are on top of things, such as turning in assignments on time and completing homework. They read material to children, have children read to them, and make learning fun. She said, "When parents don't get involved, then children don't receive those important principles and the effects spill over in adulthood. Those children often have a difficult time holding jobs and paying bills on time, and usually depend on federal assistance."

A father of five children—two grown, two in college, and one on the way to college—felt that a parent has to want to be empowered. "The empowerment comes from whatever the parents' desires are; if the parents want to be involved, they will go to the meetings, activities, and school events. In other words, parents empower themselves. When they step away, they give all the decisions about their child to the school, which may not be a good thing."

Parents perceived that just showing up and being seen at the school and the school knowing that they are caring parents is powerful. The parent of a college student said, "The schools need to know that they want to be a part of the educational process in a positive way and are not there to call the teacher a liar and cuss administration. I feel that parents should go to the school to be supportive. Parents are empowered by being there."

There are many reasons parents gave for not being there for their children. However, they agreed that all stakeholders are responsible when a child fails. Most parents shared that the utmost responsibility for the success of the children belongs to them. The next chapter will give insight into this important discussion.

CHAPTER FOUR

RESPONSIBILITIES

Whose fault is it when a child fails in school? Parents feel that the school, community, home, church—all the stakeholders and the child each play a role in the child's success and that each must be held accountable when he fails. During our discussions, parents felt that they need to own their children's education. Three of the parent's perspectives concerning this issue are as follows:

"Teachers do the educating, but it is on the parents to make sure the education is being effective for their children."

"Discipline at home is important because if the parents cannot control the child at home and make him do his homework etc., than what chance does the school have in the classroom?"

"Whatever the parent's value, the children will value, because parents are the only example some of them see. I am an educator, so I lead by example so that my children will value education. They were not given a choice as to whether or not they are going to college . . . I told them, 'You may not want to go to college but you are going from here.' I feel that it is my responsibility to enforce this value in them and not let them drift through life."

When it pertains to children, responsibility comes in many forms. One parent felt that discouraging and negative words that are spoken to a child can have a lasting, devastating effect. She felt that when teachers make prejudgments about a child's social and economic environment, this can be responsible for a student having a failing attitude.

This parent shared a situation involving a high school counselor who told a student who wanted to be a doctor that she could not because there were none in her family. She felt that this remark discouraged the young lady and was responsible for the student's decision to drop out of school. She stated, "I feel that everyone who has connection with the student should feel some responsibility for her success. Words are powerful."

One parent's thought was that: "In a broad sense, there is often a correlation between the level of education and income. I think that when it is a generational thing, such as generational poverty, it is hard to break, but no matter what your economic situation is, the family is still responsible for the success or failure of its children. They will need more support but they also have a responsibility to seek out the support they need."

Meeting the needs of her three children is a challenge for one parent. This parent expressed her need by saying, "It would be very helpful for teachers to provide parents with information on how they can engage in learning activities with their child in the home, using everyday situations. They can communicate this through e-mail, newsletters, etc. Parents should also initiate these discussions with their teachers.

PTA groups are so focused on fundraising now. Perhaps a return to discussions on how parents can best be involved in their children's education is in order. It is the responsibility of parents to continue to inquire of their children about their school day, review their homework, look at their assignments and textbooks, and use teachable moments to relate everyday life to what their children are learning in school."

A parent of a child diagnosed with attention deficit hyperactive disorder (ADHD) commented that she asked her son's school for help with her child because she did not know what to do or how to handle a child with ADHD. She said the school was not able to provide her with assistance. She feels that schools should be responsible by providing a variety of parenting classes and family involvement activities. She felt that the interaction a parent has with the child at home is linked with how the child responds with adults and his peers at school so it would be helpful for the school and home be consistent in modifying a child's behavior. She also felt that: "Maybe parents would have a more productive link with the schools if they felt that they were working together for the good of the whole child."

The home is responsible for making sure children have their school materials, such as pencils and notebooks. Another parent said, "parents should give their children the emotional support they need. When a parent is emotionally missing in their children's education, their children feel lost. They do not care about their schoolwork because they feel that no one at home cares. You can't teach a child who doesn't have the desire to learn; that is something that should be reinforced at home."

Do parents realize how important this emotional link with their children's educational process is? Do they need support and training in the basic daily needs of a child?

Schools take for granted that parents are making sure children are getting enough rest at night and are well fed. Parents felt that they should be doing such things, as well as keeping children safe by knowing where they are and monitoring their friends, but that this is not always happening.

Parents felt that the parents are ultimately responsible; they also feel that there are no failures just symptoms of problems. One parent summed it up by commenting, "Academic success starts at home and then it flows with them through school. If parents set the standards from day one, the student will know what the expectations are. When a student fails, the parents, principal, and teacher need to take a close look to see why this happened and what can be done to get the child on the right track or in the right school."

Another observation was that parents who are not involved with their children's education should also be charged fees and the money should be given to the school to help with programs. An example: parents who miss parent-teacher conferences multiple times without a valid reason.

The parent who made this observation commented that: "If all stakeholders were involved, it would allow for all thoughts, ideas, suggestions, problems, and solutions to be utilized in bringing up a successful child. Everyone who has contact with a child shares in the responsibility. If the child fails, we've all had a hand in the failure if no one saw warning signs and did nothing about it. Parents especially should know if their child is successful at school, and if the child is not learning, then they should do whatever is needed to improve the child's learning situation at home and at school. Parents should never stop being held responsible for their children's educational progress."

A high school principal and parent shared that he has witnessed parents giving up responsibility of their high school children. They start to decrease responsibility in middle school, he said, but in elementary they feel that "this is my baby," so they sometimes hold themselves more responsible than they hold the school. His perspective was that: "Whether or not parents feel responsible has a lot to do with parents feeling that children are more independent in high school. They may feel this way because they are tired from the challenges that come with having adolescent children. I have found that when a male child reaches ten to twelve years of age, single mothers feel that they need more help controlling him and will hold the school more responsible for the academic and social behavior of the child."

Another parent said that she felt responsible for her child not finishing high school because she did not finish. She is fifty seven years old and is currently enrolled in an adult high school, attempting to earn a diploma. She is one of six girls raised by a single mom. She shared that her mother did not push education on her children. She was okay as long as they made a passing grade: a D. She also shared that her mother just wanted them out of school; she did not care if they finished high school because she knew that she could not send them to college.

"My mother felt that her responsibility was to feed the family; she did this by working two jobs. She did not get her high school diploma, but she did a good job raising us without an education. We never went to jail or did drugs. She taught us morals, values, and ethics. We were taught how to talk to adults, how to treat people, and how to be polite. The mothers in the neighborhood felt that it was their responsibility to educate the girls by teaching us things like how to set the table, sew, and knit. My family let the children make their own decisions about education. I hold myself responsible for getting pregnant and quitting school in the tenth grade."

This parent also shared that she had three children. One of her children did not finish high school and he stayed in trouble. She said, 'It was hard to encourage him to finish school because he knew that she didn't finish. When I decided to go back to school to get my diploma, my son came back with me, and I am so proud of him. We both are at home trying to do homework and asking each other questions. Sometimes my other children, his brother and sister, help us. I feel that my going back to school has had a positive effect on my children, just like my quitting school had a negative effect on them. I would also like to think that my example to go back to school at my age is responsible for encouraging my son to value education now while he is still young."

Another perspective of parents was that parents sometimes hold the child's friends responsible. They find ways to blame their child's bad social behavior on his friends.

One father of a teenager said that he has heard parents say, "If he wasn't hanging with that bad boy in his school, he wouldn't do the things he does. The truth of the matter is that it is the responsibility of the parents to train their child how to choose the right friends. This is a part of his social development."

The parent of four-year-old girl who will start school in the next year felt there is a huge disconnection between the family and the school and that this may be because the family unit does not seem to be an important part of society anymore. He said, "Some parents look at the school as a daycare and a way to get their children out of their hair . . . kids are on their own to try to figure out and navigate their way through the education system and sometimes even life."

Another parent viewpoint concerning being responsible was that: "For the most part, if parents are missing out on their kid's education, the parent is to blame. Schools give parents many opportunities to play an active role; parents too often don't make it a priority. I personally feel that it is a shared responsibility between parents and the school and community. The school has a job to do, but parents should be their backup; that means turning off the television and cell phones and working together with the child. It also takes the full community supporting the success of the child."

Having discussions with parents concerning their children's education was an interesting journey. As I spoke with the parents, I began to categorize their comments. I then used the different categories to create a summary of our discussions.

CHAPTER FIVE

SUMMING UP THE DISCUSSIONS

I am bringing *Missing Link?* to a close by summing up the discussions I had with parents. It is my hope that this type of open dialogue with parents will not end. I felt that it was important that parents were not restricted or influenced in the way they responded during our conversations. My desire was to gain their true perspectives about the educational process of their children and what they felt their role was in it.

Many questions developed from the conversations, and I found that getting parents to share how they felt by discussing the questions that emerged has proven to be a valuable way for them to communicate their perspectives. Common responses to the questions were put into categories; the categories were used to make summations about the conversations. As a result parents of different social and economic status have shared and can continue to learn from each other's experiences. Several conclusions can be gleaned by summing up the overall perspectives that parents shared.

From the discussions we find that parents need to be empowered and to do so they need to be informed. They need to be included to play an active, effective role in the educational process of their children. This may mean providing resources and the support parent's need, such as time-management and parenting classes, which will ensure that parents are equipped with necessary tools.

Parents will need to be there playing an active role in their child's education to guarantee that all children are receiving what they need to be successful academically and socially. Communication is the key.

Parents also felt that they need to find ways that will make their presence in the schools a positive link, because when all stakeholders link together, a strong chain of success is formed for the students. The community, home, church, and school should form a chain that can support the students and keep them from being bound by failure. To be successful, none of the links can be missing. Weak links also need to be identified and strengthened.

Another shared thought was to hold them more accountable. Parents cannot let life challenges and their personal endeavors keep them from knowing what is going on with their children. They realize that they cannot always wait for schools to offer them the support system they need.

They determined that they have to seek and request the type of support they need.

Parents feel that a support system should be set up, especially for the new generation of parents. When new parents compared themselves to their parents, they were sometimes confused about what to do concerning the educational process of their children; they were also concerned about causing more harm than good. Many parents felt that parenting classes are needed to help sort through some of the Meth and to give them more security about how to support their children in all aspects of life.

We are what we think . . . we accomplish what we know we can . . . education is important and should be given priority—how parents feel about these thoughts and many more influence how children feel and also sets the ground work for their success and failure. Parents feel strongly that school teachers and administrators should not assume that because parents are low-income that they do not care about their child's education. Support systems and conversations need to happen for parents of all ethnic and social economic stations in life.

As I spoke with parents of different cultural and economic backgrounds, they all expressed that at times there are life challenges that they face that prevent them from giving their children's education their full attention. Parents of higher economic status are sometimes more invested in their children's education and therefore are more involved with monitoring their investment by making sure their children are being educated in the best possible way. Parents who are less invested and overwhelmed with everyday survival feel that if their children are fed and have clothes to wear to school that the school should appreciate their efforts, and if the children do not perform in school it is on the teachers and the school to support them.

Until educators truly communicate and understand the perspectives of parents, they will continue to make the determination that parents are the missing link—but are they?

Most all of the parents I spoke with also felt that parents were missing in the educational process of their children in some way. Some parents were satisfied with their role and felt that because they defined their role differently from the school system that the school did not feel that they were doing enough; the parents felt they were doing all that they could. A small number of parents blamed themselves for not being truly linked or even caring enough to be linked to their children's education. They felt that they had enough to worry about just getting through day-to-day concerns and survival.

"I no longer have an us-against-them mentality," said one parent, "and I see the importance that all the links have in supporting our children's education. When one link is weak or missing, we all pay the price because if children are unsuccessful, they will become a burden on their parents and society."

Parents also shared that having the discussions helped them reflect on their involvement in their children's education and the importance of staying connected with their overall academic and social development. After our discussions, parents expressed that they were very thankful for the chance to talk openly about how they feel. Some of them felt that the discussions helped them to reevaluate whether or not they are linked to the educational process of their children.

It is my desire that parents will read *Missing Link?* and know that it is okay to ask questions and have conversations with other parents and with those educating their children. There is much more to be learned from listening to the perspectives of parents.

NOTES

Interview questions were created by the author to encourage and motivate conversations with parents. The responses to the questions became the discussion topics for the chapters of the book *Missing Link?* No methodical circumstances were used; however, a method was created by the author to share parent responses in an organized and accurate manner for the reader. Parent quotes were not transcribed. The author took notes, redirected questions, and used open-ended questioning to glean parent perspectives.

The following are some of the interview questions used to develop topics for parent discussions.

How do a parent's feelings about education affect how their children feel about education?

Why do you feel that parents' link with their children's school is less after elementary school, or is it less?

Do you feel that there is a difference in how low-income versus high-income parents view their children's education?

Do you feel that parents are missing in the educational process of their children?

In what ways can you, as the parent, be empowered?

About the Author

MATTIE LEE SOLOMON, PHD, has contributed to the education of the children in Indianapolis, Indiana, for over twenty years. As an educator and life learner, she has over fifteen years of experience as a teacher and school administrator. Dr. Solomon earned a K-12 Business Education Teacher degree from the University of Indianapolis; a master's degree in Educational Administration from Ball State University, Muncie, Indiana; and a PhD in the Philosophy of Education from Indiana State University, Terra Haute, Indiana. Her experience as an educator provided many opportunities to communicate with hundreds of parents about the education of their children. This experience inspired her to write *Missing Link?* as a tool that can be used to encourage parents to share their perspective about the educational process of their children and their role in it. Dr. Solomon is currently retired from school administration but continues to work with secondary education.